DIARY OF A
CONFUSED EDUCATOR

(PART 1)

Ashanti Branch, M.Ed.

DEDICATION

This book is dedicated to my first teacher, Glenna Goodman Hamilton, my mother, who did the best she could to shield me from the chaotic world of Oakland, California; who always found a way to stretch a dollar, and who I dearly love.

This is for my siblings who allowed me to be their first teacher. Whether they chose to allow it or it was taken by force, I was the first. I thank you, Tara, Keron, and Henry Isaac for giving me those lessons that continue to feed me today.

This is also dedicated to the profession of engineering that let me lend my talents to the study, the execution, and the delivery of not only many, many construction plans, but many, many buildings and features around the country. I'm grateful to all of my mentors, teachers, educators who were and are a part of this journey. This is a compilation of all the lessons I've learned, piled together in this one soul, and trying to put it back out in the world the best way I can.

To the young men of the Ever Forward Club, starting with the founders in 2004 at San Lorenzo High School to the most recent young men's health groups in the San Francisco Unified School District, thank you for your voices. Thank you for sharing your thoughts, your needs. To the teachers who I worked with, thank you for your time, attention, and presence in my career. Thank you for sponsoring our young men to attend their field trips and fundraisers and for volunteering at our events.

And last but not least, this book is dedicated to the more than 85,000 people around the world who have taken a moment, a minute, three minutes to create a mask. I am grateful for you. This book is not explicitly about the mask, but it has and always will be a part of the journey, and it will definitely be a part of the next book too. Ever Forward.

Hey you... yes, you... this is dedicated to YOU also!

TABLE OF CONTENTS

PREFACE

To celebrate the Ever Forward Club's 21 years of impact Ashanti Branch chronicles his stories of challenge, perseverance, mentorship, local and global impact. With a meaningful mix of passion and purpose, this is his journey of being called to education.

About the Ever Forward Club®

Founded in 2004, the Ever Forward Club (www.everforwardclub.org) mentors underserved middle and high school youth by providing them with safe, brave communities that build character and transform lives. The Ever Forward Club was featured in a documentary called The Mask You Live In, in 2015, and shortly after, led to the creation of a global self-reflection tool called the #MillionMaskMovement (www.millionmask.org) and other community building programs. The Ever Forward Club supports at-risk teens to achieve their goals, both inside and outside the classroom.

The Ever Forward Club's mission is to address the underlying causes of dropout rates, youth violence, and the growing achievement gap through mentoring and social-emotional development.

INTRODUCTION

I've been trying to write this introduction for weeks but haven't been able to find my way in. It's connected to this confusion I have as an educator; a journey I've been on for 21 years. Really it's a journey of 50 years, but being called into education is by far the most important part of that journey. It's been 21 years since the Ever Forward Club began, and as I sit here on Culver Boulevard in Los Angeles getting ready to present tomorrow at the Rare Beauty Mental Health Summit, I realize how grateful I am to introduce this journey to you.

This book will tell you how it all started. How being a teacher was not my plan—it was planned for me. Having my mom in college and being the oldest child meant teaching my siblings, and requiring myself to do it with no complaints. This means teaching has been a part of me since the beginning. The problem was that I didn't see it making me the money that I knew I wanted to make, so it was never a profession that I was going to go after myself.

When I was an engineering student at Cal Poly, San Luis Obispo, looking back, I believe the call started then, but anytime someone would tell me I should be a teacher, I would feel almost insulted because I didn't grow up with a huge respect for the profession. My plan was to be an engineer and make a lot of money. However, anytime high school students came to Cal Poly to do tours, if I had time, I would do the tour. I would offer words of encouragement, I would walk them to the dorms, I would make the tour spectacular because even then, I believed in the power of education to change lives. I still do despite the fact that, at the moment of this writing, the Department of Education is under attack.

So many things happening right now are confusing. Just as confusing as so many moments have been over these 21 years of education, not to mention the whole of my life. Looking back on these moments is what you'll find in the pages ahead.

This isn't complex or fancy book. It's a diary of confusions, questions, chaos and the travels of an educator raised by an educator. It's written like I'm telling the story first person, as opposed to reflecting on it as it was happening, but that's been the journey of my work as an educator. This book has come through many iterations. It was originally going to come out in 2024 as a celebration of 20 years of the Ever Forward Club. but so many things happened to me as an educator, and as a person who has dedicated his life to giving others as much as possible, and more. When that it didn't happen, I thought I'd just add one more story and make it 21 years, 21 stories. That didn't sound right either, because the journey never feels finished.

I put so many other things of this project. Even today as I began to finish this intro, phone calls and text messages were coming from people in my world that needed my attention. I wanted to tell them to figure it out themselves. But I didn't.

I'm learning more and more about my role as a mentor, an educator, a leader. I've learned that I sometimes set myself up for the pressure to hold it all by not giving people the chance to hold it themselves. And so as I write this introduction, I want you to know that what's ahead in this book is a reflection of that. It's worry, stress, achievement, doubt, fear, ambition, chaos, and definitely confusion. At times, it may not make a lot of sense (most diaries don't). You may read it and think it should be more polished, but it's not. It's not meant to be polished because these last 21 years haven't been. I want you to feel it the same way I did.

Coming from an engineering career where most things work, are organized, step-by-step, progressing logically toward an understood goal, it was a culture shock to land in education. You think, what in the world is going on here? Is this even supposed to happen? Was this designed not to work? Are we not going to do anything about the fact that it's not working?

In this book, you'll see that 21 years ago, a teacher found himself at the end of his rope. What would it be like to find yourself doing a job that you didn't necessarily choose, but that when it shows up, it feels exactly right?

There's no complaining about it, only acknowledging it. And that's why we're here in these pages.

Know that this is just part one. Part two will be about the #MillionMask movement, the journey of million masks that we are on right now. As of today, as I write this, we have reached 85,000 masks. I thought we would be at a 100,000 years ago, but I'm clearer today than ever before that every person who goes to that website (millionmask.org) or grabs a postcard and writes their six words of self-reflection, every mask, it is one step closer to our goal. One step at a time; one mask, one emotion, one new person with the ability to speak about how they really feel in a healthy, safe way.

I know what it feels like to try and change something important, to build something big.

That's what this book is about. If you are a teacher, a social entrepreneur, an emotional development leader, if you're a counselor, a psychologist, a therapist, a mentor, a coach— whatever you do to serve others in a system that seems unmovable—this is written to encourage you, inspire you, and hopefully push you to keep going.

Most days I look up and I feel I'm so far from my goal, but if I work to be a little bit kinder to myself, if I talk to myself the way I talk to the young men I mentor, if I encourage myself in the same way that gives me so much benefit encouraging others, here's what I would say: Ashanti, you're doing a good job.

All any of us can do is try to make this world better, and I hope that those that follow in my path, whether their experience was net positive or not, they knew it came from a place of trying to help others.

I hope that as you read this, you will want to know more. You will come and find us. You will follow our social media. You will join our community of advocates. You will stay engaged. You will become a donor. You'll become a philanthropic partner. You will join our board. You will become an advisor. I hope that it pushes you not to stay still, because our world needs more people who have come alive in it.

That's what Howard Thurman said, *"Don't ask what the world needs. Ask what makes you come alive, and go do that, because what the world needs is more people who have come alive."*

I am eternally grateful to have found what makes me come alive. Enjoy the Diary of a Confused Educator.

- Ashanti DeLamus Branch, M.Ed.

1

BE A MAN

My dad died three months before I was born. I have his last name and one photo of him. I've been told he was a loving, kind, and big-hearted man.

I was raised by a single mother on welfare in Oakland, California. At a very young age, before my mom remarried, I was told that I was the man of the house, and that's who I needed to be. Where and when I grew up, showing emotions as a man was not accepted, which meant that I was always too emotional, not tough enough, not strong enough, and not cool enough.

I think that for most of my life, I felt like something was missing from that time, and as I heal from the baggage, the wounds, and complications, I begin to see that what was missing was childhood itself. Not a lot of opportunity for the freedom and joy of a childhood when you're the primary caretaker for your siblings; when you're the 'man of the house.'

I cooked, cleaned, nurtured. I learned what adults would recognize as responsibility. But on the playground, that nurturing behavior wasn't cool. As my peers called me soft, I learned to shut off who I was deep down inside so that I could become tough.

There are so many things I wish could have been different, so many things that might have made this journey of trying to be my own version of a loving, big-hearted man in the world simpler. At every turn, and with every lesson I've learned along the way, I continually go back to that little boy and tell him, "You're enough. There's nothing wrong with you. Your start was hard. Don't compare yourself to anyone else."

Feeling like I had to 'man up' or 'be a man' before I was the age where one is usually considered a man wasn't unique to me. Our young men today are getting the same message. Peer groups, social media, and our culture itself create the conditions that pressure young men to hide their more empathic feelings and to 'be cool' instead of smart.

It's that kind of message that cut me off from myself; a relationship I've spent decades trying to rebuild. It's keeping all young men as only half our true selves. What we need now more than ever, is men who are emotionally whole, mentally strong, and who value compassion.

Looking back, I am so grateful for the journey I have been on to rediscover the essence of who I am. In those final three months of my development in the womb as my mom passed down to me the deep emotions of sadness, grief, worry, stress, and fear, I have come to realize that what she did for me was rooted in a deep sense of love for my father. Her love for him blessed me with a big heart that loves people. A soul that desires for people to achieve their best lives, regardless of where they start out. It has been a beautiful puzzle looking back over these years to see how all the pieces have come together. This season of my life, I am working on loving myself as much as I love others.

*   *   *

On December 18, 2024, my 50th birthday, my mother handed me a book. She wrote and made it by hand. She described it as a book of secrets from before I was born and in some of my early years of life.

The story you are going to read below is from that book. She has held onto this story for over 50 years. What a strong woman.

Ashanti's Book Of Life
by Glenna Goodman Hamilton

Today is Thursday, August 22, 2024, 5:10am. Ashanti, today I woke up early and decided to put the memories about life leading up to your birth on paper. Your dad came back from burying his father in Arkansas and he was really sad and very disappointed with how the Branch family behaved.

Delta said that at the grave site it seemed that his father was talking to him. I was living in Alvingroom Court, not far from Minister Reem's church on MacArthur Blvd. It was a little walk into the complex to get to my apartment but I still had my 1963 Chevrolet "Belair" that your granddaddy bought for me. My first car.

Well Ashanti, I remember calling Delta about something and he made me so angry that I packed a small bag, called Debbie in Sacramento and told her I was getting a Greyhound bus and coming to visit her for the weekend. I didn't tell Delta where I was going because I was angry with him. While I was in Sacramento that same night, your Daddy used a combination of drugs and overdosed listening to his so-called friends, they brought Delta to my house but I was gone so they took him to your grandmother Mrs. Smith's house and she called the ambulance for him.

I always wondered why they didn't take him to the hospital, maybe fear of arrest for drug use could have been the cause. Then

I thought, what if I had given Delta a key? They would probably have left him in my apartment and I could have come home Sunday and found him there, and possibly lost you, Ashanti, from the shock. Ashanti, after I got home Sunday one of your dad's barber friends came over to tell me that Delta was dead and told me what happened. Ashanti, I just cried and cried! My love, my first real love of my life gone. He left me and you alone. I kept questioning why? He didn't have to use those drugs. He wouldn't listen to me and stop because we had a baby coming into this world.

Ashanti, I was six months pregnant with you when Delta died. I felt many battles were probably going on in his mind with the death of his father. Who knows what all was going on inside him with their relationship. I just never really knew, but I know he used to rub my big belly and sometimes lay his head on you.

I never knew about Delta's relationship with God but I know he loved kids and he was happy about me being pregnant with you, and he was bragging to your momother (my mom's mother) about me being in college and how smart I was.

So education was important to him too. Ashanti, you have a lot of your dad's good qualities; God's wisdom, love of helping others, calm voice. Ashanti, I'm going to stop now. I was pregnant and still going to college. More to come...

Educator, ask yourself:

What parts of myself have I hidden or downplayed in order to fit in or fulfill a role?

What kind of person would I be, if my opinion was the only opinion that mattered?

2

THE PIVOT: ENGINEER TO EDUCATOR

(2004)

By the time I was in high school, I was putting all my energy into my education. It was going to be my way out of Oakland.

I wanted to be successful, rich, and in control of my life. I studied engineering at Cal Poly San Luis Obispo and began my career in construction. I was a man—building things, fixing things, and making money. It was the path I chose, the one I was on, and exactly where I planned to stay.

An engineer friend of mine who was teaching math at Upward Bound in Oakland, reached out to ask if I wanted to teach math on Saturday mornings. I said no at first—Friday night was one of only two nights per week that I could have fun, and I fully took advantage of my time for fun on the weekends—but after he shared that so many students would have no math instructor for the Saturday Academy, I told him that I would do it for two months but he needed to find another teacher. I ended up tutoring math at Upward Bound for more than two years.

Working with those students sparked something in me. Initially, I wanted to ignore that spark—after all, I was on a path to success, riches and control; the path I had planned for.

But that spark quickly turned into a burning call. These students needed the kind of help I needed when I was their age.

And I couldn't deny that this space felt more like home than construction. It wasn't long before I resigned from my career as an engineer and went back to school to get my teaching credential, and my Masters in Education.

My first job on this new path was teaching math at San Lorenzo High School in 2004. At first, I was the tough teacher who was going to get these kids to learn, no matter what—a warm enforcer and disciplinarian. It became clear early on that most would rather fight with me than work with me. I recognized the push-back behavior—these kids were putting on a show for their peers. They were living out the same story I was told in my youth: be cool, not smart.

As a result, young men of color were falling behind and failing. These kids were smart but unmotivated but I knew first-hand some of the challenges they were facing. Their story was my own, and they were getting the same message everywhere they went: Don't show your emotions. Don't be vulnerable. Be a man. Deal with it in silence.

However, becoming a teacher had reminded me of who I was beneath the hard shell of masculinity that I learned to wear in my childhood. In that classroom, the shell had started to crack, and I was motivated to invite these young men crack their own. There I was, after decades, becoming Ashanti the nurturer again.

If students were failing my class, it meant I was failing as their teacher. So, after realizing that there was no way the type of transformation I was envisioning was going to happen in math class, I decided to invite some of them to a special meeting that they were selected to attend. During that meeting, I explained to them that I wanted then to help me become a better teacher by joining this club. When they walked in I told them why they were here: "In exchange for lunch, I want you to teach me to be a better teacher." I told them exactly what I saw, that there was greatness in them, and I needed their guidance to help them see it themselves.

What began as one-hour lunch meetings with eight or nine students started to grow. First a few more students, then a club of over 75 students in just two years. We called it The Ever Forward Club (EFC).

This was a safe space for them to have difficult conversations, to express themselves, and to learn life lessons. We listened to each other, shared, and were able to identify the emotional masks we were wearing around school. Although we did not officially begin using the mask as a metaphor for another 9 years, young men heard other young men talking about what was happening in their lives, acknowledging where they struggled, and learning how to ask for help. In the beginning, we focused on their academic struggles; it quickly became a much deeper experience.

In 2005 we started a unique community service event called the 24-Hour Relay Challenge

And in 2006 we took our first SoCal College Tour to provide a positive incentive for young men to keep showing up, and to start thinking about their lives beyond high school.

The EFC today works with both middle and high school students in programs reaching youth and communities across the nation and around the world, focusing on positively impacting the trajectory of their futures. To this end, the EFC builds safe ways to have difficult conversations, establish trust, create deeper connections through peer-to-peer and peer-to-mentor dialogues, and provide mental health support in the students' everyday surroundings.

We work with youth to set goals and identify opportunities to meet those goals while breaking down the isolation and loneliness that teens are facing. 100% of our organization's youth graduate from high school and more than 90% go on to college, military, trade school, or entrepreneurship.

Getting off the engineering path and into the education space taught me an invaluable life lesson and a lesson about education.

Everyone has a difference to make in this world if they are given the right guidance, and the safe space to express themselves.

It was a hell of a pivot.

Educator, ask yourself:

What do I want for myself?

What matters to me and WHY do I want it? That's where the value lies.

How can connecting with others help me understand and realize my goals?

3

MY STUDENT & THE ASB

(2006)

Without meaning to, schools can sometimes create structures and environments that make it very difficult to support their most underserved students.

An example of this was a young man who was part of the Ever Forward Club was tasked with representing EFC at Associated Student Body (ASB) meetings each month, as well as managing the forms and our event space for an upcoming event.

During an ASB meeting, a teacher in charge dismissed and disrespected this student for not having the paperwork filled out correctly. The student made efforts to address the mistake himself but was still met with rejection and shame, reflecting a broader issue of inflexible school thinking and processes.

After this meeting he arrived in my classroom somewhat early, before lunch was over, completely fuming. This young man faced more than his share of challenges in life, in school, and in the world. He wasn't the kind to put up with a whole lot of nonsense from anyone, especially when it came to respect. When he came back, he said something like, "I ain't ever going back to another one of those f*cking meetings…"

Branch: Wow, wow, wow what happened?

Young Man: She gonna disrespect me like that in front of all those ASB kids.

Branch: Give me some details

Young Man: She said since we missed some of the information on the form that our event was cancelled.

Branch: Is the meeting over?

Young Man: No, I left early. She tried to embarrass me in front of everyone.

As he told me what happened I could tell it was more than just a teacher talking smack to him. Normally, he would not tolerate that from anyone, but he knew how important it was that we completed that paperwork, and he wanted to do a good job. This was about trying something new and getting disrespected which, if not handled correctly, could ruin the motivation of facing those fears again.

I made it clear that I was going to support him through this conflict.

Branch: Grab the paperwork. Let's go.

Together, we walked back over to the classroom where the ASB meeting had just wrapped up and I asked to have a word with the teacher. After dealing with a little bit of disrespect myself, I told her that my student deserved the same respect as any other student and that we needed our form approved because we were operating under a youth development program—all our events were critical to building community. As she told me that I did not have any power, I informed here that EFC was not operating like other social clubs on campus. We needed alternatives so that bureaucratic hurdles wouldn't block our students' initiatives. As teachers and staff, our job is to facilitate and uplift, not to obstruct and demean. I was angry, but respectful.

4

THREE PARAGRAPHS

(2007)

Part of our agreement in the Ever Forward Club was that if home was too challenging a place to get homework done, students could come to my classroom after school and do their homework there. And students always came to my class after school.

One afternoon, a young man came in and sat down to work on an essay. While he worked, I was preparing for the next day, cleaning up and organizing. The students never bothered me when they were there after hours, and unless they needed something from me, I didn't bother them—unless I was feeling silly and wanted to have some fun.

The student worked for maybe 15 minutes, then he packed up his bag and turned to me before leaving.

Student: I'm done and heading home.

Ashanti: There's no way you finished writing that fast.

Student: Yeah, I did and I already finished. My teacher told me I only have to write three paragraphs

Ashanti: There's no such thing as a three-paragraph essay.

Student: No, for real, it's true.

Though I wanted to believe him, I was still going to confirm his story, so I picked up the phone and called the teacher who assigned the essay. They confirmed what this young man was saying and went a step further. "I know that he struggles to write," they said, "So I told him that he only needs to turn in three paragraphs."

Okay then, I hung up the phone. I was happy the student had told me the truth but unhappy about something else. I looked over at him and he started talking.

Student: See, I told you. I told you.

Ashanti: Yeah, you're right. I sure appreciate you telling me the truth. Now have a seat. You're going to redo the essay. You aren't going to allow someone to accept less of you.

Student: (Gives me a frustrated look).

Ashanti: If you can write three paragraphs, you can write five. Doesn't matter if it's hard, don't let somebody expect less of you. Your development is going to be hard. Your growth is going to be hard. Growing is taking those hard things and making them easier.

The young man sat back down to work and rewrote his essay.

I don't blame the teacher, in fact I'm thankful for them. They were doing the best they could at the moment to help this young man. It was my job to make sure that he held himself to higher standards than what others expected of him so that he could be his best self.

Young Man, don't let anyone expect less of you than they would expect from their own child. I know it's not always but you can do hard things.

Educator, ask yourself:

What's my "five paragraphs" story?

Am I more likely to be like the student or Branch in this scenario?

What am I in the habit of expecting from myself?

5

FULBRIGHT FELLOWSHIP IN INDIA

(June 2007 - January 2008)

One of the places that always intrigued me was India. The intricacies, the stimulation of sight and sound, the patterns, the food and of course, the education system. As a first-year math teacher at San Lorenzo High, I heard about a teacher who had gotten a Fulbright Fellowship to teach in England. The seed was planted and I intended to help it grow.

In 2007, after teaching for a few years at San Lorenzo and launching the EFC, I applied for the Fulbright Fellowship to teach in India. I was so curious and wanted to learn their special sauce for producing so many engineers, scientists and doctors. I needed to figure out what was happening over there so that I could bring it back to my school, my community, and the youth in my classroom.

I arrived in Chennai, Tamil Nadu, India (formerly Madras) in late June, 2007, as part of a teacher exchange program. I traded classrooms with an Indian math teacher. For six months, she taught my class at San Lorenzo High School, and I taught her class in Chennai at Padma Seshadri Bala Bhavan PSBB.

From the first moments of that first day, I was in awe. Respect for educators was built-in to their day-to-day. The teacher waits at the door for the students to walk in, then a class leader gets the class ready to greet the teacher, and the teacher then participates with a greeting from the students.

The students say: "Sri Gurubhyo Namaha." This is a traditional respectful salutation to the Guru, acknowledging the role of teachers and mentors in one's life which roughly translates to "Teacher, thank you for coming to our class to teach us."

The teacher responds: "Sukhi Bhava." Which means, "May you be happy" or "Be happy," a wish for well-being and positive emotions.

And then the teacher enters, and the class begins…

That first day, after the special greeting, the class leader introduced me to our "Class Topper," a title earned for having the highest score on the latest math test. When this young man stood up, the class went wild, cheering, screaming and banging on their desks. I didn't know if I should run and hide or if they were playing some kind of joke on me. But it was no joke.

As a kid, I got used to hiding my math scores from my peers, so you can imagine how new this was to me. Here, this kid was recognized and praised by his peers for his excellent score; for being smart. Here, it was the coolest thing to be the smartest kid.

In that classroom, it was clear that education meant something. I wanted to capture this energy, this possibility for upward mobility, for my students back home. I wanted them to cheer and go crazy for the kid with the highest math score.

After that first day, and over the course of the next six months, I was determined to learn everything I could to bring some of India back to my classroom. If I could give them that love and fire for learning, I could show them how to bring that quote from Malcolm X to life, "Education is your passport to the future, for tomorrow belongs to those who prepare for it today."

Educator, ask yourself:

How would it feel to be seen and celebrated for the parts of yourself you downplay or hide?

In what ways can you begin celebrating others?

ASHANTI BRANCH, M.ED.

6

LEAVING SAN LORENZO HIGH

(2008)

Back at San Lorenzo High School, the teacher I had exchanged classes with had a very difficult time. Used to the respect and eager students that I was experiencing over in India, she faced the opposite. I had tried to prepare her as best I could, but there was nothing I could have said or done that would have prepared her well enough.

The Ever Forward Club also suffered while I was away for that semester. The teacher who had originally agreed to step up and lead did neither. The student president was frustrated with the kids who stopped showing up and they were frustrated with him.

The EFC needed a lot of work to get back up on its feet and at the same time, the high school had a new principal who didn't believe in or support the mission of EFC. They put up roadblocks and unnecessary red tape at every opportunity and to this day, I'm not sure why. All I know is that she made efforts not just to create a hostile work environment for me, but to stop our club's last few activities for the school year. The SoCal College Tour and 24-Hour Relay still happened, but without her support.

Once the club was back up and running, it became obvious that she had no intention of changing her level of support or the working conditions. I was still on an educational high from my experience in India and excited about the possibility of schools being transformed so that students could thrive, but for my own mental health and wellness, it was time for me to leave San Lorenzo High School.

I didn't want to. I almost had tenure teaching my favorite subject in the world and I was there because I was called to be there. I didn't want to leave my students either. I wanted to keep teaching them, keep mentoring them. It was a hard and slow decision to make.

Eventually I was recruited as a person of color to be a math specialist for an independent school and slowly began transitioning. I found a teacher who would really step up this time and support the Ever Forward Club at San Lorenzo. If I hadn't, I don't think I could have left.

At the start of summer 2008, the conversation with my students was one of the hardest I've ever had. They understood why I had to leave, and I made it clear that my passion and dedication to them wasn't ending, just evolving. I wasn't leaving because of them. I will never forget that moment. Looking into their sad eyes. But I had promised those kids that we would still do a college trip the next year, and thankfully the new teacher leading it worked with me to make it happen.

The blessing in disguise was that leaving the EFC in the care of another teacher at San Lorenzo High showed me that I didn't have to be present for the club to exist.

Educator, ask yourself:

What have I left behind me, even if it was difficult, and what do I carry forward from it?

What kind of legacy do I want to create?

7

MARIN TO OAKLAND

(2010)

At first, I was only planning on taking a one-year leave of absence from San Lorenzo High (kinda hoping the principal would leave and I could go back to resume the work I had started there with the EFC). However, one year quickly turned into two, working as a Math Specialist at St. Mark's School (now known as Mark Day School) in San Rafael, CA (Marin County) from 2008-2010.

Being at St. Mark's was like being in Disneyland. It was an educator's paradise. Everyone was so friendly. The staff berated birthdays with a continental breakfast once a month. I had a stipend for supplies, conferences, support and resources. The students were eager and there were some amazing electives like music, art and a Maker Space. This was a new world for me and I could have stayed forever. But then again, I couldn't.

I became a teacher to help and teach the underserved, not the kids who would be just fine without me. As much as I was enjoying it, driving from Oakland to Marin every day, into this idyllic setting, my heart was pulling me back to Oakland, back to my calling. Teaching at St. Mark's let me experience what it felt like to be an educator in a highly functional school, and it was amazing.

While I was there, the Ever Forward Club was experiencing some growing pains at the foundation site, San Lorenzo High School (where I was still doing my best to support Mr. Santillan who had taken over as the mentor), and also at a charter school in Oakland called Arise High School. I heard about a math position opening up there, where underserved kids would need what I brought to the table. So here I was, having first taught at a public high school, then an independent school, and now I was heading back to Oakland, to a charter school where the Ever Forward Club was already established by an amazing educator named Devin.

Devin was a humanities teacher at Arise who was working with a group of young men who had to retake the ninth grade. When I was still at St. Mark's, the co-founder and co-principal of Arise reached out to me about Devin's work with these young men, and I asked him if he wanted to collaborate. He was very open to it and I had supported him in getting the Arise chapter of EFC off the ground. Once I took the teaching position at Arise, we got to work on the EFC as colleagues. For the first time, I had a partner to work with, bounce ideas off of and dream big as to where were could take it. We were able to grow the learning and programs. The club was thriving.

I was at Arise from 2010-2012. They were good years, but something wasn't feeling right. As a math educator, I was committed to supporting students earn whatever grade they dreamed of achieving but I had followed a teacher didn't. I began to see that their grading system and my value system were not aligned. A student was more than a grade, more than a statistic or number. So in 2012, I once again followed my conviction and belief, and decided to take a position as dean at my Alma Mater, Fremont High School in Oakland.

Educator, ask yourself:

Have I experienced an environment or relationship that seemed like it "should" be perfect, but felt "off"?

What tipped me off to the discrepancy?

What feeling or instinct am I following if I leave?

8

THE MASK YOU LIVE IN

(2015)

The Ever Forward Club was invited to join the national conversation around healthy masculinity by participating in the 2015 documentary, *The Mask You Live In.*

When the filmmakers reached out to me in 2013 to spotlight EFC's work, I was working at Fremont High School in the Oakland USD, where I had graduated 20 years prior. This time, however, I was in a dean position directing the student support, affectionately called the ASAP Center of the school. I had been trying, without much success, to get some of these young men on a better track through all the activities and programs of the Ever Forward Club. So I gave the filmmakers a list of other schools where the EFC was going strong and having a major impact. In the end, they wanted to focus on where I was at that moment. They were aware that I had been struggling with this group of young men and they were prepared to see me work with them on opening up and building connection.

Then I had an idea. Since these young men found it so difficult to talk about their feelings, what if instead of asking them to talk about it, I had them write it down anonymously instead. In front of the film crew, for the first time ever, I asked a handful of struggling young men to write down their feelings on paper.

Together, each of us (myself included) anonymously wrote our emotions on a printed piece of paper with an illustration of a mask on it. On the front of the mask, I had them write down what they let people see. Behind the mask, on the back of the paper, I asked them to write down what they don't let people see. Since we were sitting in a circle, I had them crumple up their pieces of paper, their emotional masks, and throw them across the circle. Each of them picked up an anonymous crumpled-up piece of paper, opened it, and read it out loud.

The words we heard from the backs of each mask were all so similar. *"Anger, sadness, pain, missing my dad..."* and the list went on. That was it. The room changed immediately and these young men were there for each other. They *saw* each other.

That was the moment I knew we had created something powerful, an activity in which the students could tap into their emotions and begin taking off their emotional masks.

It was the birth of the Taking Off the Mask Workshop, which became the #100kMasks Challenge in 2017, and then the #MillionMaskMovement in 2020.

You can find the documentary *The Mask You Live In* on KANOPY. The trailer and the scene described above are on YouTube in a clip called: **The Mask You Live In - Teacher Clip.**

Educator, ask yourself:

What would I write on the front of my mask? On the back?

How would it feel to read what others have written, and to hear someone else read mine?

What do I expect the masks would share?

What do I expect would be unique to mine?

9

SUICIDE LETTER

(2015)

It was March 4, 2015; a day I will never forget. We were hosting a fundraiser later that night, which was the screening of the documentary *The Mask You Live In* at the HUB in Oakland; we were planning on having a great day.

I was the vice principal at Montera Middle School in Oakland USD at the time, and I had taken the day off to prepare for our big event. Our school had scheduled 5th grade tours for the day and I was needed on campus for the morning tours. After the tour, I was in my office packing up to leave when I got a call from the front office letting me know that a young man was waiting to see me.

I knew that he and his mom planned on coming to the screening that night, so my first thought was maybe he needed extra tickets. He came into my office, saw that I was packing up and handed me a letter. He said, "I see you're packing up, I'm gonna go back to class," and turned to leave. I had never gotten a letter as an assistant principal and rarely ever gone one as a teacher, so I asked him to stay while I opened it.

I've read the words written on that sheet of paper so many times, they're ingrained in my mind:

"Dear Mom, Mr. Branch, and Family, I'm planning to kill myself today, tomorrow, or the next day..."

The letter outlined his plans. Plans he had put so much thought into that it felt like there was no way I could persuade him not to go through with it.

The day slammed to a stop. With my bags packed and one foot out the door, everything paused, stood still. Quiet. I looked at him. His eyes were fixed on the floor.

All the training, all the case studies you read, none of it prepares you for this. I knew the rules and I knew what to do to protect myself from getting sued, but emotionally? Emotionally, I was lost. I didn't know what to say or do. I was wracking my brains. This was the first time a student had handed me a suicide letter.

"Okay," I eventually managed. "Have a seat. This is going to be a tough day. This is going to be a rough day. But I got you. I got you. I'm here."

The protocols in a situation like this are designed around liability, not empathy, comfort, and care. I sat there with him, told him I would support him through this, and I kept him by my side. We were each other's shadows until his parents and the authorities arrived. The situation felt so pressurized. It was tough to see him being driven away in the police car. He wasn't being arrested but they needed to take him in to get him the care and evaluation he needed.

That day became a sad memory filed somewhere in my hippocampus. When he returned to school a few weeks later, all of the teachers knew he had a "golden pass" to come to my office whenever he needed. I'm not sure why my name was on the letter, but he must have trusted me enough to at least tell me what he was planning.

At the end of the year he came to my office again with another letter.

"Ok, let's go have a seat," I said, thinking *oh no, not again.*

"No, I'm good," he said. Yeah, I'm good."

This letter began differently:

"Dear Mr. branch: I wanna thank you for being there for me. If it wasn't for you I probably wouldn't be here right know..."

I keep the words of those two letters close to everything I do. They continue to inspire me, and remind me of the stakes. So many young men don't know where to go, where to look for someone who can just hold the space for them. Someone to help make things better, not worse. I'm beyond thankful that he trusted me.

Educator, ask yourself:

Do I have a person in whom I can place deep, high-stakes trust?

Do I desire to be that person for someone else?

10

FROM D.SCHOOL TO FULL-TIME AT EFC

(2016)

During my second year as the vice-principal of Montera Middle School, I heard about a fellowship at the Stanford d.school for mid-career professionals who were restless in their careers and wanted to use design thinking to turn their ideas into reality. I was chosen to be a K12 Lab Education Fellow at Stanford's Hasso Plattner Institute of Design from 2015-2016. I wanted to grow the Ever Forward Club and I needed to figure out how. The experience there was empowering and the result was that I pivoted from working with the EFC as a side job to leading it full-time.

In this fellowship I learned a design thinking framework that helped to expand the work of the EFC and go after the dream of scaling it up. Working with the eight other fellows in the program, we workshopped our ideas and visions to make them our realities.

Studying and exploring with design thinking was a game-changer not just for the club, but in my life as well. Design thinking is also known as Human-Centered Design, which means taking a human-centered approach to problem-solving that emphasizes understanding needs, ideating creative solutions, and iterating on those ideas. It requires empathy, collaboration, and experimentation. I was learning how to strategically and practically develop procedures for the growth of an organization. Real-world skills for real-world impact.

To get EFC to where I knew I wanted to take it and where we are now, I needed to dedicate myself 100% to the organization. That meant leaving the day-to-day work of an educator, as well as my administrator position at Montera Middle School. It was another tough decision, but it was clear this was my next chapter.

I began doing Taking Off the Mask workshops all over the Bay Area and around the world. The work of the Ever Forward Club was ready to move to the next level but as I was finishing the fellowship in 2016, we still didn't have a funder for the program to help it grow.

My mentor asked me how much money I had saved, my burn rate, and how long we could last with my savings. I calculated that we had three months for myself, a part-time COO, and a program coordinator. He said, "OK, why don't you just go for it for three months? And if you don't find money in the next three months, then go back to get a job. You're an experienced math teacher. You're an administrator. There are plenty of job openings in the middle of the year that will be glad to have you apply. So if you really want this dream, go for it?"

So I did. I took that leap with those first three months in the fall of 2016 and I've been the full-time Executive Director ever since. Every day I'm aware that this is exactly what I'm meant to be doing—not to have this title, but to be doing this work. This October will be nine years of me doing it full-time. As we continue to grow, scale, and develop new products and resources for the community and our schools, it's the result of my soul's work. I do it with passion and gratitude.

Educator, ask yourself:

What feels like the work I should be doing?

What type of activities and tasks fill me with passion?

What makes me feel joy?

11

THE PHONE CALL THAT CHANGED IT ALL

(2016-2017)

In 2016, the Ever Forward Club was at Claremont Middle School working with After School All Stars. We had a classroom and taught a social-emotional leadership course. One day, just before the class was about to start, the phone rang.

"Hello," said the voice. "Hey, you know, I just wanted to tell you that your activity makes the classroom very unsafe." I was very confused, with no idea what the person was talking about.

"I don't think I understand. What makes the class unsafe?"

The voice on the other end of the call replied, "Well, I did the activity that you did in the documentary, The Mask You Live In, with my students and it made the classroom unsafe."

WOW. I had no idea what to say.

The sarcastic, hard-working, passionate, take no sh*t jerk in me wanted to say, 'This is your fault for thinking that this was actually done in just three minutes. After watching a three-minute clip without any instruction, you tried to recreate it with your students without understanding the bigger context of the work.'

That's exactly what this educator had done; they tried to replicate hours and days and weeks of trust-building in a few short minutes. I had relationships with those young men in the documentary. I knew them as their dean, and as a mentor invested

49

in their success, one who deeply cared about each of them. We're asking these youth to share important, sometimes scary things about themselves.

Thankfully, the teacher, educator, engineer, designer in me realized that I needed to learn from this tension.

All I could do was focus on the words of this concerned educator. Unsafe? What were they trying to do? What was their objective?

Then something occurred to me. If this person is willing to call me and tell me that the activity didn't work for them, I'm sure there are many other teachers out there who are watching that three-minute clip and assuming that was all there was to it, then trying it with their own students. They would be making the same mistakes and blaming me in silence.

You can't build that kind of trust and safety in three minutes. You can't build a house without a foundation.

The documentary had accidentally made the activity look easy. But it wasn't. What people saw on screen was the result of more work and compassion than can be measured.

Making an unsafe environment is literally the opposite of the activity's purpose when translated and executed correctly.

As I empathized with this teacher's situation even deeper, I began to worry that teachers and educators were going to try to recreate those three minutes from the documentary, which meant that we would have to teach them how to do it the right way. My biggest concern at the time was now that we had finally created something that was uniquely ours, what would it mean to give it away without figuring out how to it could financially benefit our small non-profit organization, which was desperately in need of raising money if we were to grow. I was only in my first few months of being a full-time Executive Director.

Shortly after that phone call, I reached out to one of my mentors to think out this idea and help me wrap my head around what had just happened. He acknowledged my feelings and pushed me into action: "What do you want, Ashanti? Do you want to be able to create impact and growth or do you want to make money?"

"I want both," I told him.

He laughed and said, "Yes, I know, but which one is most important to you right now?"

The ego answer was still both, but I knew the biggest goal is rooted in my purpose to help youth build character and transform their lives. I wanted to continue to have an impact on these young men and women.

He responded with the sentence I did not want, but needed, to hear. "Then you've got to give it away." So that's exactly what we did.

We expanded our team and began planning the launch of a movement by providing our activities for free, with instructions on how to safely do them with youth and/or adults. With this purpose-driven pivot, I trusted that eventually, financial stability would show up.

Educator, ask yourself:

Where have I "missed the foundations"?

Where have I misunderstood or misused tools or lessons, even if my intentions were good, because I was trying to do things more quickly or easily?

What wisdom do I have to give away?

12

THE BIRTH OF THE MOVEMENT

(2017)

It was October 2017 and I was pumped. I had prepared my speech for my team and I was ready for a movement. A Million Mask Movement.

I wanted to share the mask activity with millions. My enthusiasm was received and then contained. My team liked the idea but even I seemed wary of the scale of a million masks. "How are we going to do that?... That's a lot," I heard them murmuring (and saying loudly).

I allowed their fear to ignite my own and I took a zero of the initial goal. We settled on 100,000 to start off and called it the #100kMasks Challenge. My internal fear and doubt stopped me from dreaming bigger.

The #100kMasks Challenge was born of the need to get our activities out there for educators and communities, in a tangible and safe way, without me needing to be physically present to facilitate. On that day in October, 2017, we launched the #100kMasks Challenge at Lake Merritt in Oakland, CA.

By 2019, the momentum had grown and we had mailed out 150,000 cards to educators around the world. Over 600 teachers and educators signed up to participate in the challenge. But even though we were sending materials out to educators, many educators weren't mailing them back. Also, mailing physical cards around the world was a logistical, customs, and financial nightmare, so we began to explore alternative solutions.

Later in 2019, the Ever Forward Club was a finalist for LinkedIn's Compassion Award, leading to an investment in our work. So we created an online platform to participate in the mask activity. This virtual tool allowed us to engage educators and schools around the world as long as they had access to the internet or a mobile phone.

As we developed the digital site and prepared for the November 2019 launch, we considered strategies to encourage people to use the digital tool, having already distributed over 180,000 mask cards worldwide. By March 2020, the COVID-19 pandemic unfolded, and the need for a digital platform skyrocketed. During a time when mental health became so important for all of us, this digital tool became vital to providing social and emotional resources for youth and adults during and after quarantine.

During the Summer of 2020, while the world was still in quarantine, the #100kMasks Challenge website grew exponentially. Realizing that there were going to be kids stuck at home during the summer months, without social interaction or outlets, I created our first internship program.

Dubbed the Social Emotional Leadership Academy, the program was mostly virtual for the summer. Students participating received a stipend, were split into teams and given two main responsibilities. The first team created our podcast called *Taking Off the Mask*. Their role was to learn how to develop and create a podcast, which we continue to use today. The second team rebranded the #100kMasks Challenge to the #MillionMaskMovement (www.millionmask.org).

The #MillionMaskMovement now has a monumental goal. We are getting ready to surpass 100,000 completed masks and want to engage 1,000,000 people worldwide in a self-reflective activity to remind them that they are not alone and #ThereIsMoreToMe than anyone can see by just looking at me.

Educator, ask yourself:

Have I ever allowed fear and doubt to influence me?

Have I ever underestimated the impact I could have?

What would happen if I allowed myself to think, dream, play, and live BIG?

13

MY MASK

When I host guests on my podcast, "Taking Off The Mask," we participate in the #MillionMaskMovement activity together. I've taken off my mask many times over the years through 220+ podcast episodes and at each of our more than 200 facilitated workshops.

I've done this so many times. Sometimes the words I use to describe my mask are words that are accurate and reflective of that day, a result of being present with my guest or who's in the room, or sometimes resonating with my guest in the moment. Over the years, however, I've seen recurring themes and emotions when I take off my emotional mask. There are three: *funny*, *serious*, and *hard-working*.

I chose the word *funny* because I like to laugh. I love humor. Growing up, I experienced what it was like to be the subject of people's jokes and it didn't feel good. So I like to make people laugh, but not at the expense of others—there's nothing better than a good belly laugh at a joke or a life situation that has opened up a lot of humor. It's good for our bodies to laugh and great for connecting with one another.

I'm also really *serious*. Even intense. My team knows this. Sometimes I accidentally mix my intenseness with humor, which makes things unclear and confusing for the people I'm working with. I might try to make things funny to lessen the intensity, but then what I'm asking for becomes unclear. Mixing those two is not good and I'm working on keeping them separate. I think our world is in need of people who are serious about making change and improving the lives of others.

I chose *hard-working* because I work hard. Starting at a young age, I felt the responsibility of taking care of my siblings and taking care of the house. I'm a hard-working adult because of my experience as a child.

On the back of my mask, the things I don't want people to know about me—those things that I try to cover up—are *fear of failure, sadness/grief about death,* and *childhood trauma.* Linked to my hard work ethic is my fear of failure. You've got to keep going, keep going, and keep going because not going means not being good enough. I'm trying to find a balance between that limiting belief that drives me to work hard, and an understanding that I'm good enough to take breaks, and look after myself.

The *sadness and grief I feel about death* are sometimes— almost always—playing behind the scenes. At some point, I thought I would just get over the death of my father if I didn't talk about him. I never met him but always felt I was missing him. I put that grief behind my mask because as a child, I didn't have a safe place to openly talk about those feelings. Growing up, my mom was very loving and caring but we didn't sit around and talk about how we felt. It was always just, "Go wash this, go clean that, finish your chores, finish your homework, take care of your sisters, go take your siblings out to play…"

Who had time to talk about the fact that I felt worried or sad or that I missed my dad? So I just held it all in, kept it all back. That *childhood trauma,* the painful things that happened to me as a kid, there was no outlet for it, no way I could talk about or process them. They are walls that I continue working to break through as an adult.

We all have these masks, and the only way to move through them is to realize that there is more to you and more everyone you meet than you can see just by looking at them. And #ThereIsMoreToYou than anyone can see just by looking at you.

Educator, ask yourself:

Where and with whom do I feel safe to take off my mask?

Is it possible to be fully loved if you are not fully known?

14

JAIME'S STORY

*"I realized that other kids were having problems too. Some
people had it worse than I did."*
- Jaime

The young men and women who have joined the Ever
Forward Club are extraordinary. The opportunity to mentor and
help these youth get onto a path that doesn't lead straight to prison
is a beautiful thing. The statistics show that it's our black and
brown youth who are the most underserved, who are dropping out
of high school, and who are most likely to end up behind bars.
When I founded the EFC, I wanted to help create better outcomes
for them, and help raise the next generation of emotionally healthy
youth.

Twenty years later, I see and experience the fruit of all that
work and mentorship in the kind of adults these young men and
women have become.

Jaime, now 33, is a perfect example of this. I first met Jaime
in 2007, shortly after I got back from India. He was a freshman at
San Lorenzo High and his mother had just died. His P.E. teacher,
Mr. Longaker, saw that this young man was suffering, so he
introduced the two of us.

Jaime has said himself that when we first met, he didn't want
to be around other people and that he wasn't dealing with his

mom's death. He was emotionally stuck with no dreams and no goals.

The first few time Longaker brought him to my class, during my prep, I asked him what time I needed to bring him back. He told me I could keep him for the period. Jaime was looking down at the ground with wardrobe and posture that told me he was disconnected. When he shook my hand, I couldn't feel any life in him. I warmly demanded that he squeeze my hand. He was sort of shocked by this. "Huh?" he said. I repeated, squeeze my hand. After that I realized two things: One, that he was very strong, and Two, he was playing very small.

Since it was my prep period and I had a lot of things to do, I thought it would be a good idea to have him go with me to run some errands, make some copies, and organize my classroom. While I made copies, I began to get to know him, asking him questions, so I was talking to him and then turning around to do stuff. I think it sometimes makes conversations with young men easier. There were several questions to just break the ice, but I wanted to know who he was so I began to ask about his family.

Branch: Do you have siblings?

Jaime: Yes, a sister and a brother.

Branch: Oh that's great, where did you move from?

Jaime: City in the Valley.

This next part of the conversation is not as clear in my memory as for the words that were said, but I will never forget the feeling and the essence of what happened next.

I only knew one small part of his story… He had just recently started school with us.

Branch: Who did you live with out there?

Jaime: My aunt.

Branch: Who do you live with here?

Jaime: My uncle.

Branch: Oh, ok, what brought you and your mom out here in the middle of the school year?

Jaime: (SILENCE)

I looked around and thought I had missed what he said. So I asked him again, "why did you come to live with your uncle?" He looked up at me with tears welling up in his eyes, and as if he was shaking off an impossible request, he shook his head from side to side, "NO".

Since I'd asked so many questions, I wasn't sure which one caused the simultaneous closure of the vocal cords and the high pressure release of the tear ducts.

Branch: Is this about your mom?

Jaime: (Nodding) Yes.

With that, my copying job was over. I knew we needed to get back to my room so we could talk in private.

For the next 20-30 minutes, that young man cried and let himself show the grief that seemed, at least to me, like he had been holding back for years.

When the bell rang, I encouraged him to go over to the sink and wash his face. I told him I was proud of him for letting so much of that out. I told him to grab a couple of snacks and I invited him to the Ever Forward Club meetings every Thursday. I added that he was welcome to come to my room any day at lunch or after school. As the days passed, he would show up each day, he began to open up. Not just with me, but with the other young men in the EFC. He started to talk and work through some of the trauma surrounding his mother's passing.

He said it was through the EFC meetings that he started to realize that his peers were also dealing with trauma and that some people had it worse than him. He says the EFC was a place for him and his peers to go, a space of support, and absolutely no judgment.

Every year, I took the club on a SoCal college tour and it was this college trip, he says, that changed his life. He began to dream again.

Jaime engaged with the college kids, asked questions, and began to think about what he wanted for his future. I told him that if this was the path he wanted, if he wanted to graduate high school and go to college, he would have to bring up his grades. And he did. He graduated high school and attended college. He didn't have it easy and he still doesn't. But he has the tools to see himself through. In his own words, if it hadn't been for the EFC and that college tour, he would never have graduated high school. He wouldn't even have tried.

Educator, ask yourself:

> How can I have more empathy or compassion for those students who are carrying around invisible burdens that visibly affect how they walk through school and life each day?

15

WHEN THE WORK IS MORE

THAN THE WORK

Mentoring outside of the classroom is very different from mentoring inside the classroom; much more personal and much more like a parent.

Outside the classroom, I've often mentored my now-godson. His mother had passed away and his abusive father was not in his life. He knew difficulty, and like so many of my students and Ever Forward Club members, he needed a role model. Someone to look up to, to teach him things, sometimes even the simplest of things, to help him through life.

My godson was in middle school, and he had the stinkiest feet. Now, I don't know if he knew that they were stinky, but they were. Every time he took off his shoes, I was like dude, what is going on? So, one day, when he was in the seventh grade, I got him some new shoes of his choice and a big pack of socks. He was so happy.

Fast forward two weeks, I ask him how his new shoes are treating him, he says they're so great, and he takes them off. His feet are stinky again! I couldn't understand. I bought him new shoes and fourteen pairs of new socks! I was so confused and blurted out, "Why are your feet so stinky again?" He looked at me and gave me a side-eye. I saw from his face and his body language that he was embarrassed.

I apologized. It took me a while to realize what was going on but when I did, I apologized. He had never been taught anything about foot hygiene, that after feet get sweaty or wet, socks need to be changed; feet need to be washed.

I asked him if he wanted to learn how and he said yes. That day, we started a simple process of teaching him how to take care of his feet and his personal hygiene. I realized that I was never taught how to take care of my feet or throw a ball, and yet from two different generations and backgrounds, we were held responsible for skills we were never taught and thus only learned when a mentor had shown up.

These simple things aren't available to kids who come up in hard circumstances. This means we need to meet young people with curiosity, and learn about where they are in their hearts and minds.

Mentorship isn't one thing. It's boots on the ground. It's time, connection, effort and care. And it's worth it.

Educator, ask yourself:

What do I wish someone had taught me when I was younger?

What knowledge do I have to share, even if it doesn't seem "important" or "unique"?

16

LORENZO'S STORY

"I would be in jail or dead by now if it wasn't for Ashanti and the Ever Forward Club."
- Lorenzo

Lorenzo has the names of his cousin and brother tattooed on his arm. Both were killed by gun violence in the same year. He's the first to say that if it weren't for the Ever Forward Club, he would be dead too.

He grew up in Oakland, hanging out with his cousin and brother, and in his own words, was headed for a thug life. I first met him when I was a teacher at San Lorenzo High. One day after school, there were a bunch of students making a bunch of noise outside of my portable, so I went to see what was going on. I saw a group of young men goofing off and being loud. I went over to ask them what they were up to. Lorenzo said he wasn't even a student at the high school but he would be coming the following year. He was hanging out, waiting for his older cousin.

"Ok," I said, "when you get her next year, I want you to join our club."

When he arrived as a freshman in 2006, he did. At the time, Lorenzo was living with his aunt and didn't know where his parents were. He had no role models and the adults who were still in his life were either in jail or on drugs. This was his norm.

He could tell that I cared, and I could see that what he really needed was a safe place. He would come to club meetings, but then he wouldn't. He did okay in school, but then he didn't. This cycle went on for a few years until the college tour. He says that he had no concept of a future for himself until that trip. Visiting those college campuses brought him outside the only life he ever knew in Oakland. I made sure he knew he could do anything he set his mind to; anything he wanted.

Lorenzo graduated and went on to college. He continued to volunteer and later worked for the Ever Forward Club for years. He now has a family of his own. He is a father. A good father. He jokes that his kids are putting him through all the stuff he put me through years ago.

For young men like Lorenzo to find inspiration and positive male role models, a safe space has to come first. The Ever Forward Club was there to provide it when he needed it most.

There is a video of Lorenzo's story on YouTube called, **Lorenzo Interview: Why EFC is important to me.** I encourage you to watch it.

Educator, ask yourself:

Where/when/with whom do I find a safe space?

Where is it possible for me to grow that space?

17

JOHNATHAN'S STORY

"In school, they don't really teach you about your emotions.
They teach you how to work, work, work. They don't really teach
you how to embrace your emotions or creativity."
- Johnathan

Before he joined the Ever Forward Club, Johnathan was very quiet and shy. He did well in school and was dedicated to his learning, but he wasn't focused on himself. He wasn't building his self-esteem or self-confidence.

In 2018, after attending a Taking Off the Mask workshop at Oakland SOL Middle School, Jonathan was intrigued and wanted more. During the pandemic a few years later, he became one of our interns for the Social Emotional Leadership Academy. He helped develop the podcast that is still going strong today, and when I hosted him on the podcast in 2023, it was a full-circle moment that moved us both.

In late 2022, Johnathan restarted the Ever Forward Club at Fremont High School, his own high school at the time. I supported and mentored him through it all, making sure that he had everything he needed to run the EFC successfully. He grew and thrived as a young leader with EFC.

Johnathan was the only young man from his school who committed to the college trip, and that's where our work really began to take on deeper meaning. Going to a club meeting is one thing, but going on a college tour is another. He got to know other young men from other schools who were also in the Ever Forward Club. This brotherhood provided him with a profound understanding of our mission and solidified his commitment to the EFC.

When asked what he has learned from the Ever Forward Club, he emphasized his growing leadership skills, his voice, and his understanding of anger. "Anger comes from hidden sadness. It's like a coping mechanism. And it's much easier to be angry than it is to be sad," he said.

When he was an intern with the Social Emotional Academy, he also helped a lot with organizing our mask cards. It was tedious work, he remembers, but he was also moved by the masks' similarities. They resonated with him.

Johnathan found his voice with the Ever Forward Club. He learned how to speak up, ask questions and lead. He is an expert on what it means to be a young man today and is now a senior at Sojourner Truth Independent Study.

He has goals and will graduate soon with the hope of attending a trade school to become a journeyman carpenter. He will take his voice, his leadership, and his growth with him into the future.

Educator, ask yourself:

What would I say if I owned the full power of my voice?

What would I do if I knew I couldn't fail?

What's worth doing even if I fail?

18

JUSTIN RELATES

"It was crazy. It was anonymous… three words on the front and three words on the back… but when you hear what other people are feeling and thinking, it was like everyone felt sympathetic for each other, everyone was there for each other."
- Justin

In 2020, at the height of the pandemic, Justin started a YouTube Channel called *Justin Relates* to try and bring awareness to teenage depression and suicide. Through quarantine, when isolation and loneliness were everywhere, it would be Justin's outlet as well as an opportunity for others to see they weren't alone. Justin had spent his life hiding his feelings, keeping them deep below the surface. He had suffered trauma, loss and painful grief, which had turned into a struggle with depression.

I first met Justin through one of the other young men I was mentoring. He was a high school senior at Encinal High School. I soon learned about his YouTube channel and his talent for filmmaking. He already knew about our work because he had watched the documentary and participated in the Taking Off the Mask workshop when he was a freshman. As a senior, he also brought the #MillionMaskMovement first to his leadership team and through an amazing sequence of events, Justin took the work of the #MillionMaskMovement forward and even brought the movement to his whole high school (and another high school down the road).

During the pandemic, we saw more masks than faces in those rare moments that we went outside into the world. These were literal masks of safety keeping us all just a little bit further from each other. To address this moment where all of us were battling feelings of loneliness and hiding behind masks, Justin partnered up with us to create a video called "Hiding Behind Our Masks." A video that powerfully captures the Mask Challenge, and how rewarding, and necessary, it is to take off our masks.

Justin has turned his struggle into a way for us all to see each other. Through creativity and courage, he has been able to bring the work of the EFC forward to make a difference in our communities and around the world.

Educator, ask yourself:

What do I expect people to have in common with me?

What have I assumed is only mine?

19

JOSHUA GAO

In 2019 at the Hive Global Leader Summit I met Joshua. He was 14, maybe 15 at the time. He was at a conference for global leaders and he was easily the youngest person in the room. He had created a company that was trying to figure out how to use sound waves to extinguish fires. That stood out to me and being a mentor of young people, I was hoping to meet him at some point.

During one of the last meals of the summit, we sat down together and connected. He talked about being a part of some leadership activities and said, "maybe I could do the mask activity."

Absolutely, I said. He had completed the Mask Challenge as a part of that conference and knew how powerful it could be.

Fast forward to 2021.

I get a text from Joshua. He had just received an email from his assistant principal with the idea of doing a Mask Challenge for his entire school—2000 students and about 500 teachers and staff. His text to me arrived on a Thursday, asking if I could get him 2500 masks by next Tuesday.

What?

After we talked about potential strategies, he went to Staples and found out that it would cost around $600 to print 2500 masks by Tuesday. That was too much money for his budget and for mine, so we came up with a plan for him to go to the store in the morning to speak directly with the store manager, show them some of the masks that kids had already done, to maybe inspire the store to sponsor the school's mask challenge by printing all 2500 cards for free. He did, and it worked! He called me after meeting with the store manager and I told him that not I'd never gotten Staples to donate 2500 masks to a school before, but he did.

Now that he had the materials he needed, the next thing I asked was who was going to help him. As a person who knows what it's like having a hard time asking for help, I saw Joshua trying to do everything by himself. I told him to call a few friends, people he trusted to help him with the work and who understood how important this was to him. So he made a few calls and gathered a good group of students to help make it happen.

After the first workshop at his school, he called to tell me about it. That was a rough moment. Some students hadn't listened and weren't taking the challenge seriously. It was a discouraging moment for Joshua and his team. I spoke with them, had them take a breath, and reminded them that every mask matters. If a student is disconnected from the idea of understanding the mask they wear, then maybe they have a pretty strong mask. I gave them a few pointers for the next day's workshop that might help spark engagement with the challenge.

He and the team called me again the next day to let me know it went and this time, it landed. "The room was dead silent," he said. "People were listening when we presented. They connected with each other. It went perfectly."

Imagine that. A handful of dedicated students came up with the idea, got their principal and school leadership on board, convinced Staples to sponsor the challenge, and then presented it to over 2500 students, teachers and staff. It was an entirely student-run experience and I'm so proud of how they pulled that together.

Joshua learned to enroll people in his passion. To show people what he's excited about and get them excited too. For me, I learned I could mentor young people from across the country (Joshua is out in New Hampshire and I'm on the west coast), I didn't have to be in the room for this work. It showed me that if you can inspire someone with your words, you change the world.

During my first conversation with Joshua, I encouraged him to make a short 1-minute video during each pivot or milestone so we could refer back to it afterwards. You can see the full story on YouTube called, **Joshua Gao: Global Champion.**

This success with Joshua has inspired two programs that we have been piloting and expanding. One is the Global Partners program where we partner with educators and leaders around the world who are looking to implement the #MillionMaskMovement globally. The other is the Masks, Emotions, and Math Project, which is a project-based learning resource for schools and youth development organizations who are looking for real-world learning experiences for their students.

Educator, ask yourself:

Who or what inspires me? If the answer is "no one", then how can I seek out inspiration?

What would I like to inspire in others?

20

GOING GLOBAL

The Ever Forward Club and the #MillionMaskMovement are now well-established, and well-traveled around the world. We have been able to bring our work from supporting just a small group of young men at a high school in San Lorenzo, CA, to an all-ages, all-genders movement that spans the globe.

In January of 2017, I traveled to Oaxaca, Mexico, to visit my godson. When I was in his village of Teotitlan del Valle, the local middle school agreed to have me come and do a mask workshop with their students. On a blank piece of paper, before the Taking Off the Mask Workshop or the #100kMasks Challenge was even codified, students in this little village created their first masks outside of the United States.

Even though my Spanish was not perfect, I understood what they were saying; we had the words to communicate emotions. The depth and richness of the vocabulary were powerful. I was really thankful to see how, even though we were working in a different language, the emotions were the same, and the need to talk about these emotions was the same.

In October of that year we officially launched the #100kMasks Challenge. In December, we took the movement and a stack of Spanish mask cards back to Mexico City. With this new tool and an official campaign, we were able to walk up to complete strangers in the zocalo, the city square in Mexico City, and make masks together. It was organic and beautiful.

Also in 2017, when I was a Fellow at Stanford, I was invited by an organization called Education For Change to attend a conference in Australia. At the same time, I was invited by the Mankind Project to attend a screening of the documentary, *The Mask You Live In,* on the Gold Coast. The timing was tight but worked out perfectly. The screening came first, then onward to Melbourne for the conference. There, I was given fifteen minutes to introduce the #100kMasks Challenge. After that we broke out into smaller workshops and did the mask activity. Educators from all over the world participated, and learned how they could bring these activities back to their communities.

In 2018, I was invited back to Australia to participate in the Queensland Administrators and Educators Conference. With about 500 educators, we did the *Taking Off the Mask* activity and I was then invited to Bray Park High School in Queensland. We did a workshop there, and my heart just opened up for those students. It was powerful to watch an entire school share what they were going through, to talk about it and make space for their own emotions.

A lot of students came up to me afterward to connect and stay in touch. There was so much more going on with some of them than anyone could ever see. Whether it was grief, worry, or sadness, these kids just needed a safe place to recognize and deal with these emotions.

After doing workshops in Mexico and Australia, it was clear that the movement was going global. In different countries, with different kids, these youth just needed a safe space to be held for them. I have since had the privilege to bring workshops and the work of the Ever Forward Club to conferences in Columbia,

Canada, New Zealand, Nigeria, Portugal, India, Romania, and Iceland. Former mentees have taken the workshops further to Brazil and Nepal.

Since developing our digital mask-making tool in 2019, the Ever Forward Club and the #MillionMaskMovement have touched the lives of participants in over thirty-five countries with close to 100,000 masks made worldwide. We continue to grow this self-reflective experience to remind youth, adults, and communities everywhere that they are not alone.

Educator, ask yourself:

Can recognize and celebrate how far you've come?

What have you achieved that the child version of you would never have dreamed?

ASHANTI BRANCH, M.ED.

EPILOGUE

In March 2024, I took eight of the young men I'm currently mentoring in the Ever Forward Club—all from different high schools—to the education conference at South by Southwest (SXSW) in Austin, TX. It was inspiring. For me, for the young men, and for the people visiting our conference stand.

EFC's interactive booth became a beacon of inspiration, captivating visitors and filling an entire wall with masks, each one telling a story of hope, struggle, and resilience. This visual testament to our collective journey towards greater authenticity, reflection and connection has left an indelible mark on all who participated.

The opportunity to share this challenge and speak live in front of an engaged audience highlighted a universal desire for authenticity and understanding.

We decided to record the conversation and presentation "What's up with young men?!" as an episode on the "Taking Off the Mask Podcast" and the result was profound. Speaking in front of approximately one hundred guests, two of our young men in the Ever Forward Club, Johnathan and Wenceslao, answered questions with openness and eloquence.

At EFC, we ask our youth a lot of questions. We ask about the feelings they let people see and what the ones they don't. We ask them how they're doing. If we don't ask what's up with our young men then as a society we keep making up stories, assumptions and form the answers ourselves. If we want to truly understand them, the only way is to ask them directly.

When we were on stage at the conference, I let Johnathan and Wenceslao do most of the talking. It was clear that both of these young men were seeking connection: connection with their peers, connection with their teachers, and connection with their communities.

As I look back on the work of the past twenty years, I see that every twist, turn and choice in my life has been centered on connection. On making safe spaces where everyone can be, feel, and grow. I didn't have that growing up, but it's my calling to make sure these young men and women do.

Twenty years of EFC reminds me of the power of community and the shared vision that binds us. Our youth today are hungry for connection and spaces where that connection can flourish. Our work is to continue the conversation, foster connections, and make an impact, one mask at a time.

So, where are we going from here?

Ever Forward.

ABOUT THE AUTHOR

Ashanti Branch is a trailblazer in education reform and youth mental health, known for creating safer, more connected schools through workshops and social-emotional learning tools. In 2004, he founded the Ever Forward Club (EFC) to tackle high dropout rates among marginalized students. After more than a decade as a math teacher, he left the classroom in 2016 to pursue the mission of the EFC and the #MillionMaskMovement full-time.

EFC combines youth mentorship with teacher development and has achieved powerful outcomes: 100% of student members graduate high school, 90% pursue higher education, and 0% have been incarcerated. The free #MillionMaskMovement (an Anthem Award winner) features over 85,000 emotional "masks" submitted by youth globally.

Ashanti's work has been featured at SXSW, on CNN's *This is Life with Lisa Ling*, *The Kelly Clarkson Show*, and in the documentary *The Mask You Live In*. A 4x TEDx speaker, Fulbright Fellow, and 2023 recipient of the U.S. Surgeon General's Medallion, Ashanti is a sought-after keynote and consultant on the youth mental health crisis.

www.ingramcontent.com/pod-product-compliance
Lightning Source LLC
Chambersburg PA
CBHW071540120626
46550CB00006B/2523